RABBITS, RABBITS & MORE RABBITS!

New and Updated

By GAIL GIBBONS

HOLIDAY HOUSE · NEW YORK

For Diane Foote

Special thanks to Sara Ketelson, of the Mammology Department, American Museum of Natural History.

Library of Congress has cataloged the prior edition as follows:

Library of Congress Cataloging-in-Publication Data

Gibbons, Gail.
Rabbits, rabbits, & more rabbits / by Gail Gibbons.—1st ed.
p. cm.
Summary: Describes different kinds of rabbits, their physical characteristics, behavior, where they live, and how to take care of them.
ISBN 0-8234-1486-8
1. Rabbits Juvenile literature. [1. Rabbits.] I. Title.
SF453.2.G53   2000
636.9'32—dc21
99-16765
CIP
ISBN 0-8234-1660-7 (pbk.)

Second Edition
ISBN: 978-0-8234-4576-9 (hardcover)

DALMATION REX

FLEMISH
GIANT

NETHERLAND
DWARF

There are wild rabbits and tame rabbits. Tame rabbits can be gentle and loving pets.

3

A FOSSIL is the hardened remains or traces of plant or animal life preserved in rock.

The first rabbit relative/cousin lived 55 million years ago and was found in Mongolia. Early rabbit cousins hopped around like today's rabbits but had smaller ears and a longer tail.

ALL MAMMALS are warm-blooded animals, and they drink milk from their mothers when they are babies.

HARE

TEETH, called INCISORS

RABBIT

Rabbits are members of the Leporidae family along with their close relatives, hares. All hares are wild. Leporids have four sharp front teeth used for gnawing. They are mammals.

COTTONTAIL RABBIT

EUROPEAN RABBIT

The two most common kinds of wild rabbits are cottontail rabbits and European common rabbits. Wild rabbits live on every continent except Antarctica. All tame rabbits are descendants of European common rabbits.

Most rabbits have the same basic characteristics.

There are big rabbits and small rabbits. Their heads can be pointed and narrow or broad and flat. Wild rabbits have short brownish fur. Domestic rabbits have short or long fur that can be white, black, gray, reddish, brown, or a mixture of these colors. Their fur keeps them warm.

Most rabbits have a splash of white on their short, fluffy tails. When a rabbit senses danger, it will use its white tail to confuse predators as it runs away.

Hop . . . hop . . . hop! Rabbits get around by using their powerful hind legs. They can also run as fast as 25 to 35 miles (40–56 kilometers) an hour. Many can leap 15 feet (4.5 meters) and can jump 1 to 2 feet straight in the air.

THUMP… THUMP…
THUMP…

Pads of coarse and compressed fur under its feet protect the rabbit's toes. These pads also give the rabbit a good grip as it leaps or runs. Often, when a rabbit senses danger it thumps a hind leg on the ground as a warning to other rabbits.

A rabbit depends most of all on its excellent hearing. It moves its ears together or one at a time to catch the sounds coming from any direction.

Rabbits can see better than people in the dark. A rabbit's eyes are on the sides of its head. Because of this, it can see to both sides as well as to the front and back. A rabbit has a good sense of smell, too. Its nose wiggles constantly as it sniffs to identify any scents.

Rabbits that live in the wild have all kinds of enemies. They are hunted by foxes, hawks, and many other animals. Their biggest enemy is people who hunt them for food and for their fur.

When an enemy appears, a rabbit may stay very still to not be noticed. Or it may run away.

Rabbits are vegetarians. That means they don't eat meat. In the spring and summer months, wild rabbits eat leafy plants like clover and grass. Biting and chewing help wear down their front teeth, which grow continuously. During the winter months, they live on bark, twigs, buds, and even pine needles.

FORM

A WARREN is a series of underground burrows and tunnels.

BURROW   TUNNEL

Cottontail rabbits nest and sleep in a shallow hole called a form in the spring and fall. During the winter, they find protection under brush or wood, or in the shelter of a ledge. The European common rabbits live in warrens of two to ten rabbits.

Rabbits are crepuscular, which means they see best and are most active at dawn and dusk. Rabbits will sleep and nap during the day and night.

DOE

BUCK

A well-cared-for pet rabbit can live eight to twelve years. In the wild a rabbit may live to be about one or two years old. A male rabbit is called a buck. A female rabbit is called a doe.

KITS, also
called KITTENS

The doe cottontail rabbit carries her young inside her body for about thirty days. Several times a year she will give birth to four to eight babies in a group called a litter. Baby rabbits are called kits or kittens.

They are born with their eyes closed and without any fur. To keep them warm, the mother covers them with grass and bits of her fur in the form, or nest, she has dug in the ground. At about a week old, the kits have opened their eyes and grown a coat of soft fur.

When they are about three weeks old, the kits leave their nest. They dig their own forms. Their mother only nurses them for the first few weeks of their lives. Then they begin to find their own food.

When they are about three months old, they begin to raise their own young.

RHINELANDER

A domestic kit is old enough to leave its mother when it is about eight weeks old. It's fun to adopt a baby rabbit or a grown rabbit for your own pet, but you must allow time to take care of it, especially since a rabbit is not an easy starter pet.

HOW TO TAKE CARE OF YOUR RABBIT

There are about 50 breeds of domestic rabbits.

Handle your rabbit gently and speak softly. Never pick up a rabbit by its ears, scruff, legs, or tail. When holding a rabbit, grasp its back with one hand and use your other hand to support its back legs. Hold it close to your body.

Your rabbit needs a place to call its own. Usually this is a rabbit cage.

A special water bottle should be hung on the side of the cage. Change the water daily.

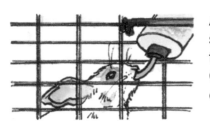

Feed your rabbit dried rabbit food twice a day. Feed it one handful of greens, vegetables, and fruit once each day, too. Rabbits love carrots, but they shouldn't have too many since they are high in sugar. No rhubarb allowed!

Always remember . . . your rabbit needs love and care.

Remember, rabbits' teeth grow constantly. They need to chew to keep their teeth worn down. A rack should be attached to a side of the cage to hold fresh alfalfa, oat hay, or timothy for the rabbit to chew. A gnawing log is good, too.

Keep your rabbit's litter box clean.

Rabbits run a lot in the wild, so your rabbit needs time outside its cage each day. Never leave it alone when it is outside its cage.

Take your rabbit to the veterinarian for its yearly checkup.

Rabbits are a social animal, so they are happiest around other rabbits. Consider adopting two rabbits.

CARING FOR AN INDOOR PET RABBIT

Your rabbit needs a cage to call its home and to sleep in. The cage needs to be big enough for your rabbit to stretch out.

Keep your rabbit's litter box in a place your rabbit can get to easily. Always keep it clean.

Line the cage with wood shavings. Change these often to keep the cage clean.

LITTER

NEVER let your rabbit chew on electrical wires!

Many people keep their rabbits as indoor pets.

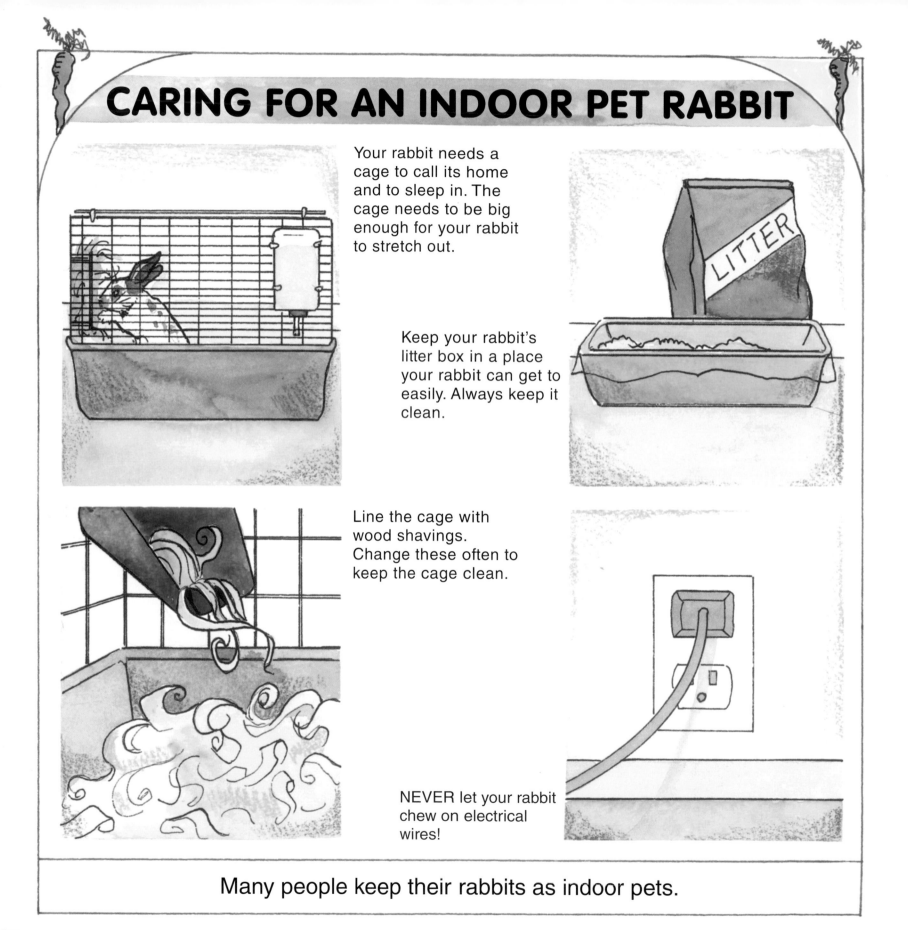

CARING FOR AN OUTDOOR PET RABBIT

A hutch must have lots of space for your rabbit to live in.

Put the hutch in a safe place away from any other animals.

Keep the hutch in the shade, away from bright sunlight.

HUTCH

Put wood shavings in the hutch to make your rabbit comfortable. Put a nest box inside the hutch. Put hay inside the nest box so your rabbit can make a bed. Clean the hutch out often. Also make sure your rabbit has enough food and water.

When it is very cold outside, bring the hutch inside to a warm and protected area.

Other people build outdoor homes, called hutches, for their rabbits.

CINNAMON RABBIT

Often, people enter their pet rabbit in shows or contests. Sometimes these are held at fairs. The rabbit that is judged to be the best wins.

Rabbits are lots of fun to watch in their natural environment. But, best of all, rabbits are fun to play with. They are wonderful pets that require lots of care, attention, and love.

A WILD RABBIT

A NEWBORN RABBIT
HAS NO FUR.

ITS EYES
ARE CLOSED.

SHORTER EARS

FUR STAYS THE SAME
COLOR YEAR ROUND.

RABBITS LIVE IN
GROUPS.

SMALLER BODY

SMALLER FEET

SHORTER LEGS

AND A HARE

A HARE

A NEWBORN HARE HAS FUR.

ITS EYES ARE OPEN.

LONGER EARS

SOMETIMES FUR TURNS WHITE DURING WINTER.

HARES LIVE ALONE.

BIGGER BODY

BIGGER FEET

LONGER LEGS

HOP . . . HOP . . . HOP . . .

NEVER try to tame a wild rabbit.

When a rabbit is very scared it can make a terrible screaming sound.

All wild rabbits' ears stand straight up. Some rabbits' ears hang down. They are called lop-eared rabbits.

When your pet rabbit is happy, it might do a binky. A binky is when a rabbit jumps in the air and does a spin.

The smallest kind of tame rabbit is the Netherland dwarf rabbit. It weighs about 2 pounds (1 kilogram).

The biggest kind of tame rabbit is the Flemish giant. It can weigh about 24 pounds (11 kilograms).

The Easter Bunny is probably the most famous legendary rabbit. A German legend tells how the Goddess of Spring turned a bird into a rabbit. The rabbit was able to lay brightly colored eggs. The goddess gave them to children as gifts. That's why we say the Easter Bunny brings eggs.

Rabbits groom themselves like cats. Unlike cats, they cannot cough up hairballs because rabbits cannot vomit.

In China it is a tradition that each year is ruled by one of twelve different animals. One of these animals is the rabbit.

Mother rabbits may make their nests in plain sight. She will also limit her time at the nest to prevent predators from finding it. So, if you see a nest full of baby rabbits with no mother, leave it alone. The mother will be back soon.